FASTBACK® Crime and Detection

Fun World

GARY BRANDNER

GLOBE FEARON
Pearson Learning Group

FASTBACK® CRIME AND DETECTION BOOKS

Beginner's Luck
The Blind Alley
Fun World
The Kid Who Sold Money
The Lottery Winner

No Loose Ends
Return Payment
The Setup
Small-Town Beat
Snowbound

Cover *t.r.* Eyewire/Getty Images, Inc.; *m.* Walter Bibikow/The Image Bank/Getty Images. All photography © Pearson Education, Inc. (PEI) unless specifically noted.

Copyright © 2004 by Pearson Education, Inc., publishing as Globe Fearon®, an imprint of Pearson Learning Group, 299 Jefferson Road, Parsippany, NJ 07054. All rights reserved. No part of this book may be reproduced or transmitted in any form or by any means, electronic or mechanical, including photocopying, recording, or by any information storage and retrieval system, without permission in writing from the publisher. For information regarding permission(s), write to Rights and Permissions Department.

Globe Fearon® and Fastback® are registered trademarks of Globe Fearon, Inc.

ISBN 0-13-024492-9
Printed in the United States of America
1 2 3 4 5 6 7 8 9 10   07 06 05 04 03

1-800-321-3106
www.pearsonlearning.com

Detective Sergeant Miles Becker was not happy. The air conditioner was broken, so it was hot and steamy in the car. His wife Rhoda was speaking to him only when she had to. And the kid in the back seat had complained for almost the whole 40-mile trip from the city.

On top of that, Becker felt he was wasting an entire day of his vacation. All in all, he was in a rotten mood.

"Are we there yet, are we there?" whined the kid again.

"I'll tell you when we're there," Becker growled without turning around.

"You don't have to be so nasty," Rhoda said. "And you might call the boy by his name. It's Kevin, in case you forgot. He *is* your nephew."

Becker flashed an evil smile in the rear-view mirror. "I'll tell you when we're there, . . . *Kevin.*" He returned his attention to the road.

Rhoda gave him a cold stare, and Kevin continued to complain for the next ten miles. Finally, Becker turned into a dusty parking lot with a sun-faded sign that read: *Welcome to Fun World! Parking $1.*

"Okay, kid, we're here."

Rhoda gave him a dirty look.

"*Kevin*, we're here," Becker said.

"It's about time," said the boy. "Why do you drive so slow?"

"Because I am a police officer sworn to uphold the law."

"You could drive fast *and* safe. You wouldn't kill anybody."

"Don't be too sure," said Becker, looking the boy in the eyes.

Rhoda gave Becker a shove to get him out of the car. The three of them crossed the unpaved lot to the Fun World entrance. They could smell popcorn and hot dogs in the light breeze. From inside the park they could hear the noisy, run-down rides carrying fun seekers up and down and around.

Inside the gate, Kevin looked around in disgust. "Sheesh! What a dump."

"Nobody promised you Disneyland," Becker said.

"It isn't much, really, is it?" Rhoda said.

"Maybe not, but it will have to do," said Becker.

Rhoda looked around at the old buildings and wheezing rides. One small building was completely covered with a green plastic tent.

"What's that?" she asked.

"They must be killing bugs or something in that building," Becker said. "Gassing the rats or cockroaches or whatever they've got."

"Isn't that dangerous?"

"Not unless somebody crawls under the tent and then breaks into the building. The law says it's got to be locked and sealed."

He looked at his nephew. "Say, Kevin, want to have some fun?"

"Miles, cut it out," Rhoda said quickly.

"I wanna see Barney Bunny," the boy announced. "He's the only good thing in this crummy place."

"Why don't you find out where he is?" Rhoda said to her husband.

Becker sighed heavily. "I'll ask somebody." He looked around, then started toward a fake Western saloon. There was a woman dancing on the stage outside it. She was wearing tights and a lot of makeup.

"Why don't you ask that man at the Ferris wheel?" Rhoda said, taking hold of Becker's arm.

Becker sighed again and walked over to the Ferris wheel ticket booth.

"Barney's off today," explained the fat man sitting there. "Fridays it's Chubby Chipmunk. His first show is in five minutes, over there in the park."

"Chubby Chipmunk is the pits," said Kevin when he heard the news.

"Well, Chubby Chipmunk is what we got," Becker said.

The "park" was a little larger than the Beckers' living room rug. There was a patch of grass, a stone bench, a fake lamp post, and a real trash can. A dozen or so people were standing around looking bored.

Ten minutes went by. At last, a sad-looking figure came dragging into the park. He was dressed in a patched and ragged animal suit. The oversized head was made of wire covered with papier-mâché. He looked like a huge, crazy gopher.

"Is that supposed to be a chipmunk?" Becker asked.

"I told you he was the pits," said his nephew.

Rhoda said, "Be quiet. Let's see what he's going to do."

What Chubby Chipmunk did was stumble into the center of the park and drop heavily onto the stone bench. Then he just sat there, with the painted face on his silly-looking head grinning at the crowd.

"Heck of an act," Becker said.

"I told you," Kevin reminded him.

"He doesn't seem very lively," Rhoda admitted.

"I'm gonna find out what his problem is," Kevin said. Before Becker could grab him, the boy ran up to the slumping figure on the bench. "Why are you just sitting there? Why don't you do something?"

The chipmunk seemed to gather his strength. He clamped a paw on the boy's shoulder. Then he leaned forward and put his face right next to Kevin's ear. The boy's eyes widened suddenly, and he ran back to his uncle and aunt, his face pale.

"What happened?" Rhoda asked.

"I asked him why didn't he do something. He told me if I didn't get away from him he *would* do something—to me."

"What did he say exactly?" Rhoda asked.

Kevin repeated what the chipmunk had said. Rhoda's mouth popped open. Becker, trying to keep a straight face, said, "Tsk-tsk."

"Can you imagine such a thing?" Rhoda demanded. "Saying that to a little boy!"

"Well . . . ," Becker began.

"Never mind," Rhoda told him. "We're going straight to whoever is in charge of this place and report it. The very *idea!*"

Becker recognized his wife's tone. He knew it was useless to argue with her. They headed for the building where the park manager had his office. And Chubby Chipmunk dragged himself off the stone bench and shuffled back in the direction he'd come from. The morning show was over.

Walter Fitzgerald was the manager of Fun World. He was a hunched little man with a big nose and bulging eyes. Sitting behind an old wooden desk, he listened patiently while Rhoda Becker made her complaint.

"That Roy Dempster," said Fitzgerald, shaking his head. "I've had trouble with him before. He's a nasty guy. I'd fire him if I could, but I'm only the manager. The owners use this place for a tax write-off. They don't care who works here, as long as they work cheap. But I'll have a talk with the chipmunk."

The office door opened, and the dancer from the fake saloon entered in a cloud of perfume. "I need a fresh costume, honey," she said to Fitzgerald. "This one's all sweated up."

"It looks OK to me," said the manager. "Besides, the others are locked in the supply shed."

"So give me the key."

"I'm supposed to keep it locked up another 12 hours," Fitzgerald said. "It might not be safe yet. And those pest control guys left some of their equipment in there."

"I don't care about that. I need a fresh costume." The woman stroked Fitzgerald under the chin with a long forefinger. "Please, honey? You want me to look nice, don't you?"

"You look great, Lu. But I'd just as soon you quit working here. Between that saloon show and your women's group in the city, I hardly ever see you."

She poked playfully at his ear. "I've got to do something. I'd go crazy just sitting around the house. Anyway, my group doesn't meet tonight. We'll make up for lost time. OK?"

Fitzgerald squirmed in his chair. "Your next show's not for four hours. I'll call the pest control place and see if it's OK for me to just run in and out."

"That's my honey," the woman said, planting a kiss on Fitzgerald's big nose.

As she walked out the door, the park manager grinned at Miles and Rhoda. "My wife Lucille," he said.

"What are you going to do about that chipmunk?" Rhoda said.

"Like I told you, I'll have a talk with Dempster."

"A lot of good that will do," Rhoda said.

"Yeah, lot of good," added Kevin.

Becker glared at the boy and started to rise from the chair.

"I don't know what else I can do," said the manager.

"My husband's a police officer," Rhoda said. "A sergeant."

12

Becker groaned.

Fitzgerald put on a big smile. He reached into a desk drawer and came up with a pack of tickets. "Tell you what, you ride on anything you like the rest of the day as my guests. At two o'clock Dempster does the afternoon chipmunk show. I promise you he'll behave better."

Becker started to refuse the tickets. But Kevin already had them clutched in his sticky little hands. As they left, Rhoda was frowning. She still wasn't convinced that the chipmunk would clean up his act.

By two o'clock Kevin had ridden the Whoopee Wheel, the Tilt-A-Whirl, the Octo-Wonder, the Thriller-

Diller, and the Whip Cracker. He hated them all. Becker had bought hot dogs, candy bars, popcorn, peanuts, and something sticky he couldn't identify. His stomach ached, his feet were sore, and his temper was ready to burst into flame. By the time they returned to the park for the afternoon chipmunk show, he was thinking of only one thing. And that was getting home to his easy chair and the ball game on television.

This time they were treated to a very lively Chubby. He clapped, he danced, he tumbled. He posed for pictures with the kiddies. He shook hands—or paws—with the adults. The children screamed with delight, and the grown-ups laughed. Even Becker caught himself smiling at some of Chubby's stunts.

"Fitzgerald must have given him some high-powered pep talk," he said.

As the chipmunk danced along the edge of the small crowd, a little girl held up a stuffed Barney Bunny toy. Chubby Chipmunk threw up his paws in pretended shock and staggered backwards. His feet tangled, and he fell on the seat of his chipmunk pants.

As the people laughed and clapped, Chubby started to get up. He got halfway to his feet, stumbled, and sat down again. He clapped the paw mittens to the large head as though he were embarrassed. The laughter grew louder. Chubby Chipmunk flopped over on his back. He kicked his fuzzy-booted feet a couple of times and then lay still.

"Now that's more like it," Rhoda said.

"Get up, Chubby," several of the children called.

Kevin joined in. "Get up, Chubby! Do some more."

But the chipmunk-suited man still did not move.

"You don't suppose he's passed out in there," Rhoda said in a whisper.

Becker shrugged.

"Why don't you go and see?"

"Why me?"

"You're a police officer."

"I'm on vacation."

"You told me a police officer is always on duty."

Becker sighed and crossed the grass toward the fallen chipmunk. When he got close to the man, he bent over and sniffed the air. His eyes narrowed. As several children started to approach, he raised a hand to warn them back. He grasped the chipmunk head and pulled, but it was fastened tightly to the rest of the suit. He felt around for snaps or zippers, but couldn't find any.

"Can I help?"

Becker looked up and saw a pale, tired-looking woman standing beside him.

"Those things are tricky to get on and off," she said. "The guys always need help." When Becker gave her a puzzled look, she added, "I'm Helen Ott, Stanley Ott's wife."

Becker looked blank.

"Mrs. Barney Bunny."

"Oh. Well, try not to breathe too deeply." He moved aside to let the woman feel around at the back of the chipmunk head.

Helen Ott gave him a strange look. She found the zipper at the back of the costume and loosened the head. She moved back and let Becker pull it off.

The people standing around gasped and stepped back, too. The face of the man in the chipmunk suit was blue. His mouth gaped, and his glassy eyes stared blankly into space.

Helen Ott screamed. "That's not Chubby Chipmunk! It's my husband!"

"Get a doctor!" Becker yelled. Somebody ran for the building at the Fun World entrance.

There was nothing the doctor could do for Barney Bunny. Stanley Ott had died only seconds after taking the fall. Becker found the cause of death in the seat of the chipmunk costume. There was a broken plastic bag tucked behind one of the many patches. The bag had contained hydrocyanic acid. When Ott sat down hard the bag had burst. This released deadly fumes into the air and caused almost instant death. The odor of the acid had remained in the cloth of the costume and the shreds of the plastic bag.

Since the cause of death clearly indicated foul play, Sergeant Becker was drafted to take charge. Young Kevin showed his first enthusiasm of the day at the thought of watching his uncle in action. His joy quickly disappeared when Becker sent him along with Rhoda to the pony ride. Now Becker would be able to keep his mind on his work.

His first move was to gather together Helen Ott, Walter Fitzgerald, and Walter's wife Lucille. The four of them paid a visit to Roy Dempster, the real Chubby Chipmunk. They found him in a trailer parked just outside Fun World. The trailer was used by employees who wanted to rest between shows. As the four approached, they could clearly hear him snoring inside.

When he was finally awakened, Dempster was shocked to hear of Barney Bunny's death. "Wow, if Stan hadn't taken the afternoon Chubby show, that would've been me!" he said.

"Were you close friends?" Becker asked.

"We went out and had a few beers sometimes."

"Like last night," Helen Ott said.

"You were out drinking with Stan Ott last night?" Becker asked.

Dempster wiped his sweaty face. He looked around at the others as though he were facing a jury. "Yes. What of it? The important thing is somebody put a bag of acid in the chipmunk suit. Somebody was trying to kill *me*. You're supposed to be a detective. How about nailing the killer before he tries again?"

Becker rolled his eyes. "I'm not Sherlock Holmes. All I'm going to do is ask a few questions to save a little time. Someone else will be taking over the case. I'm on vacation."

"Cops shouldn't have vacations," Dempster muttered.

"Suppose you tell me how Stanley Ott happened to be in the chipmunk suit this afternoon," Becker said.

Dempster's eyes slid over the faces of the people in the trailer. "I wasn't feeling so hot this morning. About noon, Fitzgerald came back and chewed me out about the morning show. He said if I didn't shape up at two o'clock, he'd make trouble for me with the owners.

"As Fitzgerald was leaving, Stan came in. Once we were alone, I reminded Stan he owed me a favor. So when I asked him to do the chipmunk show this afternoon, he said OK."

"Where was the costume at the time?" Becker asked.

"I had it hanging out back on the clothesline. That's where I air it out overnight and between shows. In this hot weather, it gets a little ripe. But who'd try to kill me? And with my own chipmunk suit?"

Sergeant Becker turned around to look at the others. "Any ideas?"

"He was never much of an act, not like the bunny," Fitzgerald said. "But that's no reason to put acid in a man's pants."

Lucille, still in the heavy makeup and the dancing costume, merely shook her head.

"Suppose Roy Dempster was not the intended victim," Becker suggested. "Suppose the killer got the right man."

"Barney Bunny?" said Fitzgerald. "My best act?"

"If somebody wanted to kill Roy Dempster, they had all night to plant the bag of acid in the costume. It wasn't in there this morning. Otherwise, it would have burst when he sat down hard on the stone bench. That means the acid bag was planted between shows."

Helen Ott was still staring at Dempster. She took a step toward him. "You said Stan owed you a favor. What was it?"

Dempster could not look her in the eyes.

"He *wasn't* out with you last night, was he?" she said. "And he wasn't out with you

23

those other nights these past several weeks, either. You've been covering for him. He was seeing another woman."

"If you two weren't together last night, it'll be fairly easy to find out," Becker said.

Roy Dempster stared silently at the floor.

"I thought so!" Color rose in Helen Ott's pale cheeks. "I figured Stan was cheating on me again. He'd been too happy lately."

The Fitzgeralds were staring at her. "You didn't . . . ," Lucille began.

"Kill Stan?" Without warning, tears spilled down Helen's cheeks. "I *loved* the rat! I could never have hurt him. Besides, I didn't know until the head came off that Stan was in the chipmunk suit."

"You knew, Roy," Lucille Fitzgerald said. "You're the only one who knew Stan was taking your place this afternoon."

"He was my pal," Dempster protested. "And where would I get a bag of that . . . whatever it was?"

"Hydrocyanic acid," Becker said. "It probably came from the building where they've killed the bugs." He turned to Lucille. "The building where you wanted to go to get your fresh costume this morning, Mrs. Fitzgerald."

"Well, I didn't get it," she said. "Hey, you're not saying it was me who killed Stan? Why would I do that?"

"Maybe because you were the other woman he was seeing," said Helen Ott. "Maybe he was going to dump you like he dumped the others." She turned to Walter Fitzgerald. "I'll bet she was out last night too, wasn't she?"

For a moment, silence lay like a heavy

blanket over the stuffy trailer. Sergeant Becker was the first to speak.

"But like you, Mrs. Ott, this woman didn't know your husband was taking Dempster's place. And it's doubtful she could have gotten into the sealed building to get the acid. I believe her husband has the only key."

They all turned to look at Walter Fitzgerald.

His bulging eyes stared back at them. "OK, so I had the key. And maybe I was ticked off with the chipmunk. But I had no reason to kill him."

"But you *did* have a reason to kill Stan." Helen Ott fixed him with her pale stare.

The little man's eyes bounced around, coming to rest on his wife. "Yeah, I knew something was going on. I never did buy that stuff about your women's group." He turned quickly to Becker. "But I didn't know who the guy was."

Becker eyed him steadily. "These walls are pretty thin. When we walked up here, we could hear Dempster snoring from ten yards away. He said that when you left here today you met Stan Ott coming in. Suppose you waited for a minute or two out in front. You would have heard them talking about where Ott was last night. And about trading off for the two o'clock show. You would have had time to go to the supply shed, get the bag of acid, and plant it in the suit."

Walter Fitzgerald turned his pleading eyes to the others, one at a time. He found no sympathy. Sinking into a chair, he said, "He may have been a great bunny. But he was a rotten man."

As Becker drove the family car back to the city, Kevin kept up another steady whine in the back seat.

"You call that fun? A bunch of crummy rides that are falling apart. Stale hot dogs. No Barney Bunny. A lousy chipmunk that gets himself killed. And the first time anything exciting happens, I have to go ride a stupid pony. Wow, I've had more fun at the dentist."

Becker smiled a little to himself. He had to admit it—the kid was right. That amusement park reminded Becker of some broken-down, out-of-date old car that had gotten lost in time. "Even the pest control guys they hired were out of touch," he thought. "It's probably been 20 years since anyone has used hydrocyanic acid to get rid of bugs."

Suddenly Becker had an idea. When he came to the next exit, he turned off the highway.

"Where are you going?" Rhoda asked.

"You heard the kid, he hasn't had any fun. We've still got time to go to Whale World."

"That place scares me," Rhoda said. "What if somebody fell into that tank with all those sharks and things?"

Miles Becker grinned and drove a little faster.

GARY BRANDNER *is the author of* The Howling, *which later became an award-winning motion picture. He has published 20 books and more than 50 short stories of horror, mystery and suspense.*